Amazon Echo User Guide

Ultimate Guide to your Amazon Echo

By Annabel Jacobs

Table of Contents

Amazon Echo looks like little more than a cylindrical speaker. The Amazon Echo is a breakthrough in the voice-powered technology. Built with the Alexa software, the device aims to follow your commands ranging from finding information to smart home management. This book will bring you to the latest attempts of Amazon in virtual interactions. Aside from Kindle eBook Reader, the Echo is an addition to the company's portfolio of devices. These devices help Amazon in determining the needs and interests of their users. This book also provides tips on how you can maintain your privacy without looking negatively towards the Echo device. Lastly, this book will give you a list of basic troubleshooting techniques that you will need to remember to guarantee the Echo speaker's efficiency.

Chapter 1: Introduction to Amazon Echo

Amazon Echo has a microphone and speaker built in a cylindrical shape that is 9 inches tall. It is designed to work as an intelligent assistant. It is similar in concept to Siri and Microsoft Cortana in that it answers questions, plays music, and performs a number of tasks.

The device is not just a speaker. It has other devices built into it. This includes 7 microphones, a woofer and tweeter, sensor array and also comes with a remote control. The woofer and tweeter help in producing better quality music, since it is also a music playing device.

Why Amazon Echo?

Amazon Echo was developed in Silicon Valley's famous lab commonly referred to as the Lab126. It is from this lab that the breakthrough Amazon Kindle devices were developed. More recently the Amazon fire TV and Fire phone were developed from this lab too, although the two did not become as successfully as the Kindle devices. What the organization is trying to do is to expand its online store, using interesting and innovative technology.

Amazon is one of the biggest online marketplaces. As far as online stores are concerned, it is one of the most recognizable brands on the internet. It has built trust over the years, and during holidays, the online store handles hundreds of transactions per second and gets about 200 million visitors per day.

Echo is designed to be part of Amazon web services. Already Amazon has a 73% of the E-reader market share through the Kindle devices. The online store has managed to be the source of both digital and tangible products for millions of online shoppers. This device could prove to be one of the most important devices that Amazon has come up with in recent years.

There are other intelligent devices that have been unveiled before Echo; notably Siri and Cortana. The difference is that Echo device makes working around the home very convenient. You may be doing repairs around the home, while requesting information from the device such as the number of inches in a foot. A house wife may request ingredients for a particular recipe, while cooking at the same time.

Inevitably, parts of the requests people will be making conveniently through Siri are purchases. These purchases may be tools, part of the ingredients, or things around the home. The shopping list makes it easier to make multiple purchases.

The fact that the device is left to remain in plugged in may seem like a disadvantage. In some ways it is. However, it makes the device hands free. You do not have to carry it around, when you are walking around the house. It has an advanced voice recognition ability that has a range of up to 40 feet.

This standalone device is about $100, making it cheaper than most of the other intelligent devices in the market. Buying a Smartphone will cost you probably, five or six times that amount. The Smartphone has limitations and doesn't possess the advanced technology.

Developing this product makes business sense for Amazon. The E-commerce industry and online purchases have grown exponentially in the last 5 years. 80% of people are either making purchases online, or researching information about products through the internet. For Amazon, this is going to be one of the things that will give the company an edge over their competitors in the near future.

The device was part of the plan by Amazon to invent an AI system that they could take advantage of to promote their products. This is probably one of the pioneering devices in home AI. In the next couple of years, real Home Artificial intelligence systems will begin to evolve into something more fascinating.

DIFFERENCES BETWEEN ECHO AND SIRI

The difference between Echo and Siri is that Echo is a dedicated device. It plays the role of a dedicated assistant. Echo is always on and you can give it commands as you go about your business around the house. For example, when cooking, you can request Echo to add items to your shopping list.

Siri comes in the form of an app on your Smartphone. An Echo app can be installed on your Smartphone or Tablet and paired with Echo. This app can be used to create or remove items on the shopping list. It may also be used to edit the voice command history.

Echo may be placed in a central location and used by anyone in the house. For this reason, some people have branded it as the

"Siri for the entire house". This clearly shows that Echo has gone one step further in as far as home tech technology is concerned.

As a home tech solution, it can be much more useful in the future, as new devices that can communicate with each other continue finding their way into the market. You can use the device to not only check room temperature, but also to adjust it using commands. It may also be used to switch off lights.

Echo does not have a screen. This may seem like a disadvantage, but it could be to discourage individuals handling it. This in turn encourages a more communal use of the device through voice commands. Use of the device is easier to coordinate when family members around the house use it.

The device is much more hands free than any mobile app could be. It is also much more convenient for home use. You do not have to constantly interact with the device or handle it to give it commands. It can be placed on any surface and will use any of its 7 microphones to detect commands.

SUPERIOR VOICE RECOGNITION TECHNOLOGY

The voice recognition technology is much more superior to other artificial intelligence assistants such as Siri and Google Now. The thing that makes Echo artificial intelligence superior is that it has far field technology unlike Siri or Google Now.

With Siri the Smartphone can only recognize your voice when you are about 1 to 5 inches from the phone. Much further than that and the device will not recognize those commands.

On the other hand, Echo will recognize your commands even when you're a few feet away from the device. It has seven microphones, which will detect the pitch, sound and process the recorded information. The algorithm has no delays and will execute commands.

STILL LEARNING

Another reason why Echo is seen as the device of the future is in its ability to *"learn"*. According to Amazon, the device keeps on learning. Every time you give it commands and requests, then cancel and request again, it begins to figure out what you like or dislike. Over time, your interactions with Echo will improve and become more seamless.

Amazon Echo has an always on feature. You can simply ask it questions as you walk around the house. It is connected to the Amazon's web services, where it constantly updates. It uses advanced algorithms to convert audio to text. It then proceeds to convert the text into questions that are fed into the cloud.

It can hear you almost anywhere you are in the room. However, your voice and distance must be reasonably high to be heard by a normal person in the same room. It connects to Amazon web services, which connects to a wide range of features, from news stories, to music and other types of apps such as calculators.

It is possible that Echo presents how we will use computers and intelligent devices in the future. This guide is meant to help maximize the use of this intelligent system. Later in the book, we will see other interesting features that we may see in the future, like switching the lights on and off and controlling temperature.

Hopefully, by learning the tricks in this guide we can bring the future closer to us.

CHAPTER 2: THE WONDERFUL FEATURES OF THE AMAZON ECHO

UNPACKING AMAZON ECHO

When you buy the device there are several things that you will get.

- Glossy box with an Orange interior.
- Cylindrical device 9.25 inches tall by 3.25 inches wide.
- Wireless and voice enabled remote control.

THE ECHO DEVICE

The device is cylindrical and measures 9 by 3 inches. It is glossy black and has in-built speakers, amplifiers and microphones. It has multiple speakers to ensure that the sounds from different parts of the house can be heard. This gives it a capability that is not possible on other intelligent devices. Even though you can speak to Siri, you can only do it while holding it next to your mouth as you speak.

The device is not portable. It needs to be constantly plugged into the AC outlet. Even though you cannot move around with it, it has two advantages. The first is that it can be given instructions while moving around, which leaves your hands free to do other tasks. The second is that the constant supply of power through the AC power outlet gives it the supply of electricity it needs to feed its always on feature.

Additionally, it needs does not have a screen and takes direct voice commands through its microphone. This ensures it is only used as an artificial intelligent assistant. Unlike, phones there are no distractions that force you to tamper with it. This leaves it free to be used conveniently by other people living in the same house.

The Echo device has LED lights located at top that indicates its status. The light can either be blue or orange. Blue indicates that the device is working properly. It flashes on and off to indicate it has received and is processing the request. The orange color indicates the device is not ready. This could happen if there is no connection to a Wi-Fi network, or if you fail to log in.

On top of the device there are a number of microphones. They are designed such that they can receive voice commands from any direction and from varying distances and still be able to process the commands.

THE REMOTE

The remote control is another device that you'll find in the box, when you unpack. It is a battery powered, voice enabled, and wireless, and can be used to pick tracks from your music play list. It has a wider range and can be used from any corner of the house to pick up commands or to control music. The remote control gives you the capability to do a number of things these includes:

- Ability to issue commands remotely from another room in the house.
- Control music playback.
- Volume control.
- Is used for activation of Amazon echo during the first install.

INITIAL SET UP OF AMAZON ECHO

1. You will need to make sure the device is plugged into a power outlet. Echo is one of the most advanced systems, when it comes to voice recognition. However, you need to ensure that it is not too close to the wall. It should at least be 8 inches from the wall to avoid echoes and reverberations that interfere with the sound.
2. If the device is properly plugged in, you will see a blue light beam spinning around the top of the device. In about 60 seconds, the light beam should then change its colour to orange and Echo will tell you it's ready for set up.
3. At this point, you may log in into your Smartphone or Tablet and install the app. You only need to simply type the URL echo.amazon.com on your device. Your mobile will then attempt to connect to Echo. Follow the steps given on the device as instructed.

4. Echo will then instruct you to put batteries into the remote that comes with it. You will need one of the buttons (as indicated on your Amazon Echo App). Once this is done successfully, Echo will turn its light to blue. You may go ahead and connect it to your home's Wi-Fi (as indicated below). If you do not need to connect to Wi-Fi, you may use the *"wake word"* **Alexa,** to begin giving instructions.

CONNECTING TO WI-FI

1. You need to note that Amazon Echo only connects to (2.5 or 5 GHz) Wi-Fi. You also need to ensure that the device has been properly plugged into the power.
2. You will need to do the connection either through the Amazon echo web app, or through your Smartphone/Tablet app.
3. Login to your account and go to Set Up a new echo under settings. If you're updating the Wi-Fi settings, you simply need to go to **Settings**, then **[Your Name]**, and then choose **Update Wi-Fi**. You may change the network or the network settings as many times as you want.
4. Ensure that the Wi-Fi network is working. Press the **Action Button** on top of the Echo device. The light will then turn from orange to blue.
5. Check your mobile or web app. After a few seconds of pressing the **Action Button**, available connections will appear.
6. Once you find the network, you only need to connect by entering your email and password.

Note: If you find that you cannot connect to Wi-Fi. You will need to do the following.

1. Check that you have plugged in the device into the socket properly. You may unplug in and plug the device in again.
2. Make sure you've registered your Amazon Echo device through the web or mobile app.
3. Ensure that the username, password and all the Wi-Fi credentials entered are correct.

Note: Echo will most likely not work with the Wi-Fi network at your workplace. According to Amazon, this is because it doesn't connect to ad-hoc networks or networks without a password. But if you have a home Wi-Fi network that requires only one password, then it should work without any problems.

BLUETOOTH CONNECTION PROBLEMS

Another related issue you may encounter is Bluetooth connection problems. Here are some of the things you could do:

1. Ensure that the device is within 30 feet of the Amazon Echo device.
2. Check that Bluetooth is turned on, in the device you need to pair it with.
3. Disconnect the Bluetooth device with the Echo device under settings.
4. Try and reconnect or pair the two devices.

MAKE SIMPLE REQUESTS

To activate Echo, and make it respond to questions, you need to use a *"wake word"*. The *"wake word"* indicates to Echo that you are giving it instructions. It helps Echo to distinguish between when you're communicating with it and when you're conversing with other people in the room.

The *"wake word"* by default is **"Alexa".** You therefore use the word **"Alexa"** before every question or request. For example, to find out who the 30th president of the United States was, you will need to structure the question as follows*, "**Alexa,** who was the 30th president of the United States?"*

NOTE: **'Alexa'** is simply the default wake word set by Echo, when you first unpack it. The only other wake word you can use at this time is **'Amazon'.**

To request Echo to play classical music simply say, *"**Alexa***, play classical music"*. Other than playing music, you can use the '**Alexa'** wake word to make other types of requests. For example, you can ask Echo to add some items you need around the house to your shopping list.

Playing Music from Other Services

By default you can play music through the Amazon music library. However, there are other options you can use. You can play music through Tune In and iHeartRadio. You can use these services by setting up the account through the Amazon web services platform for Echo that you can access for free online.

Tune In and iHeartRadio were native apps built into the Echo system. It is now possible to integrate Amazon Echo with Spotify, Pandora, and iTunes. You will however need an IOS phone, or a 5.0+ Android device to play music through these services. All you have to do is to pair the device via Bluetooth and use the commands mentioned above to play music.

UPLOADING YOUR OWN MUSIC ON AMAZON ECHO

Even though Amazon Echo application has been restrictive in doing some things like adding your own music, it is still possible to add your own personal collection of music from elsewhere. You cannot use SD Cards or flash disk devices to play music through the main device. However, there is a way you can go round this.

You can add your own MP3s, rather than listening to music that is available through Amazon Prime, TuneIn, or iHeartRadio ,which may have music that is not to your taste. You can do this by uploading the music to the cloud. The cloud has space for about 250 Mp3s all for free. After uploading to the cloud, you will now be able to play music through the device.

POD CASTS

Using the three stations that are currently available, you can do a lot, if you use a number of commands. You can play a mix of different genres, or play an artist's song through these stations.

To play a mix of songs based on artists, or genre use this command: *'Alex, Play my {artist or genre} on {station}'* for example, *'Alexa, Play Rock music on iHeartRadio'* or *'Alexa, Play R&B music on Pandora'*. Note: This is currently possible only through iHeartRadio and Pandora.

You can also tell **Alexa** which songs you like, and which one you do not like. This helps Echo to determine what to play for you in the future. This feature is only available through iHeartRadio and Pandora. To tell **Alexa**, which songs you like simply say, *'Alexa, I don't like this song'* or *'Alexa, I like this song'*

It is possible to tell **Alexa** when you're tired of a song. If you say, *'Alexa, I am tired of this song'*. This will remove the song that is currently playing from the playlist. It will also not play the song in the near future.

Other Commands related to playing music you could use are:

'Alexa, make a station for {Artist}'. A station for a particular artist will be created.

'Alexa, skip this song'. Song currently playing will be skipped.

MUTE

Echo listens to conversations within its vicinity. This is because it is constantly looking out for the wake word, which may be '*Alexa*' or '*Amazon*'.

To mute the device so that it does not respond to any command or request, simply press the **Mute** button at the top.

FLASH BRIEFING

If you like being up to date with what is going on around the world and in your local area, you'll definitely like flash briefing.

You may ask Echo to play a short briefing by simply saying *"**Alexa,** what's my flash briefing?"* or *"**Alexa**, what is in the news"*. It will give you a summary of the day's top news stories. You can listen to this as you walk to the shower, or as your prepare to go to work.

You can customize your flash news by going to flash briefing under the settings option on your web app. You can choose your favorite news network, such as BBC, or CNN. You may also choose your favorite category such as Music, Politics, sports ETC.

ADDING ITEMS TO YOUR SHOPPING LIST/ TO DO

LIST

To add peanut butter to the shopping list simply say, *"Alexa, add peanut butter to my shopping list"*. You may also add to your shopping list through the Echo app that you can install on your Tablet or Smartphone.

You can still view the items on your shopping list on the Smartphone/ Tablet app. You may also ask Echo to read out the items on the shopping list using the wake word. For example, *"Alexa, what's on my shopping list?"*, if you want it to stop, say *"Alexa, stop"*. You can make Echo stop any request in this manner.

EDITING/REMOVING ITEMS ON YOUR SHOPPING/

TO DO LIST

To edit or remove items on the shopping/ to do list can be complicated by simply using voice commands. For this reason, you can only use the app to add or remove any of the items on that list.

SETTING THE ALARM

You can set an alarm or reminder to wake you up in the morning. The alarm may be in the form of some music or flash news briefing.

1. To set the alarm you may simply use this command *"**Alexa,** Wake me up at [time]"*.
2. To stop the alarm, *"**Alexa,** stop the alarm"*.
3. To cancel an alarm that has already been set, *"**Alexa** cancel the alarm"*.
4. To snooze, "**Alexa**."

Note: you may also use the Amazon Echo app to change the settings. It has a lot of options and may be more convenient, if you want to change the settings quickly.

SETTING TIMERS

Setting the times is as simple as setting the alarm. You can set timers for when you want to cook or bake something within the time indicated by the recipe. You simply tell Echo the period of time the timer should last. You can either do this through the web app, mobile app, or through commands.

COUNTDOWN TIMER (MAXIMUM TIME 24 HOURS)

- To set the time simply use the following command, *"Alexa, set timer for [amount of time]"* (Amount of time could be 30 minutes, 3 hours or even 24 hours).
- Another option is *"Alexa, set timer for [time]".*
- To stop the countdown timer: *"Alexa, stop the timer".*
- To cancel the countdown, *"Alexa, cancel the timer".*
- To know how much time left, *"Alexa how much time is left on my timer?"*
- You can only pause the timer through the mobile app.

WEATHER INFORMATION

Amazon Echo uses Accuweather to keep information up to date. The information is updated every half an hour. It is therefore quite accurate. You can use the following commands to check the weather:

1. Local weather in your location: *"Alexa, what is the weather?"*
2. Weather in a certain location e.g. Miami. *"Alexa, what is the weather in Miami?"*
3. Find out if it will rain tomorrow. *"Alexa, will it [rain/snow] tomorrow?"*
4. Future weather: *"Alexa, what is the weather this weekend?"*/ *"Alexa, what is the weather for next Tuesday?"*

TRAFFIC INFORMATION

Another interesting application of the Amazon Echo is finding how your commute will be and discovering the best route. Echo in conjunction with HERE (formerly Ovi maps by Nokia) work together to provide up to date information.

This feature can only be used for one route and appears to be under development. It can however be useful for both an individual and the family, who use a certain route regularly. They can always find out how the route is before they leave the house.

TRAFFIC SETTINGS

1. You will need to get into the Amazon Echo App settings first before you can use this feature.
2. Go to settings then to Traffic.
3. Change the address and enter destination. This will be recognized as your commute by the Echo app.

-

TO REQUEST TRAFFIC INFORMATION

You can use the following commands:

*"**Alexa**, how is the traffic?"*

*"**Alexa**, how is traffic like right now?"*

*"**Alexa**, how is my commute?"*

Having Fun with Alexa

Echo is a home intelligent assistant that is designed for the whole family. Therefore Amazon decided to add games and interesting information that will make Echo fun for the whole family. Since Echo is always on, here are some of the things that could make it fun for the whole family.

Flip a Coin

If you are finding it hard to make a decision on what to eat for dinner, or which movie to watch, just as **Alexa** to flip a coin.

*"**Alexa**, flip a coin"* (**Alexa** will either return heads or tail).

Simon Says

The Simon says feature will force Echo to repeat the words you speak into it. It can be used to seek help, prank people and for other fun games. It filters out some of the explicit words you speak into it.

Command:

To use the Simon says feature, use the following command

*"**Alexa**, Simon says + words you want it to repeat"*

There are a number of ways you can use this feature.

- **Ask for help from another room**: You can use the remote to call for help from any room in the house. If you accidentally lock yourself in a room, or hurt yourself in the garage, this feature can come in handy.
- **Prank friends**: Using the remote you can prank friends, who are not aware of this feature. From the next room, you could command Echo to appear as though it recognizes your friend. For example, you could force it to repeat words like *"Hi Anne, you look lovely in that red dress"*. To do this, you will have to use this command; ***"Alexa, Simon says**, 'Hi Anne, you look lovely in that red dress.'"* You may need to practice a little bit to make sure you get it right when repeating the prank.
- **Other Games**: There are many other games that kids will invent once they learn to use the command. Luckily, Echo has a very good voice recognition feature.
-

HOW TO MAKE ALEXA READ OUT ARTICLES

The application has the capability to store the information on everything that you have asked it in the past. If you need to recheck the questions for the purpose of assessing its ability to answer, the questions will be available through its database.

You may also compel it to seek more information from online sources such as Wikipedia. Wikipedia has a very well organized and simplified way of presenting information. This makes it easier for the echo application to extract and read information from it.

You can use it if you want an article of Wikipedia to be read out aloud to you by '*Alexa*'. To make **Alexa** read out an article, you have to give it the command in this format; '*Alexa: Wikipedia, some topic.* For example, if you want it to read out a Wikipedia article on Mastitis, simple say, '*Alexa: Wikipedia, Mastitis.*'

Usually, Amazon will read the first paragraph of the article. This is usually enough, when you're looking for general information about a given subject. You can make it read more than just the first paragraph by simply saying *"More", "Read more"* or *"Tell me more"*. If you keep repeating these words, Echo will read the entire article for you.

MORE INFORMATION

If you want to know the age, or any other piece of information about a public figure, you can easily get it from **Alexa**. If you ask, *"Alexa, how old is lady gaga?"* **Alexa** will respond with the age of the celebrity.

CONTROLLING DEVICES REMOTELY

In most of the futuristic movies that have featured devices like Echo, the device is able to perform a wide range of functions. One feature that seems to interest most people is the ability to use voice commands to turn off lights or heaters around the house.

The initial release from Amazon was very simple and primitive.

It was probably Amazon's way to test the viability of the device in the market. Now the company has, in conjunction with other partners like Philips Hue integration and Belkin WeMo, made it possible to switch devices on and off with voice commands.

This feature is quite useful and can help to save power. The easier and more convenient it is to switch the lights, the more likely that people living in that house are likely to do it. With remote controlled switch lights in the backyard, they can be switched from the living room. Echo makes it possible to switch off these lights, while you are seated on the couch watching a movie.

With Philips Hue Integrated and Belkin's WeMo installed, you can walk in your house and command **Alexa** to switch on the lights. The commands are in a similar format to all others. *"Alexa, turn on the lights"*. If you want to switch the bedroom lights on, you simply state *"Alexa, turn on the bedroom lights."*

You can also schedule devices to switch on at a given time. You may need to switch on a fan, lamp, or security lights at a certain time of day or night. There are devices designed for this. However, Echo makes it possible to do this for multiple devices from one place online, or in mobile applications. You can set up the devices successfully in matter of minutes. You need to buy these switches for the system described to function. Fortunately, this can be bought for under $40.

Amazon is still developing the technology. There are many wireless devices that are in the market. However, the Philips Hue integrated and Belkin's WeMo are the only devices that are officially designed to work with Echo.

WHAT YOU NEED TO KNOW ABOUT SHIPPING

AMAZON ECHO

You need to be careful, when changing shipping information. You may complicate the logistics and this can make you to receive the device months after you ordered. There are two main situations where it is unwise to change your shipping date or address:

- If you had not scheduled when to receive Amazon Echo, and the shipping process has started.
- Changing shipping date to an earlier date.

Amazon has pointed out that there are still many people, who have requested the device and are still on the waiting list. Changing shipping information could potentially cause logistical challenges on their side.

According to some customers, changing the shipping address delayed the delivery of their device for months. It is advisable to contact customer support, if you need to change the address. This is a safer way to do it, if you want to avoid hitches and delays during shipping.

To change the Information through the web app take the following quick steps:

- Go to the Menu and choose 'Your Subscribed and Saved Items.'
- Choose Edit delivery date
- Change the date and the information accordingly.

- After you hit confirm, the information will be updated.

VOICE TRAINING

You can train the device to understand and to process your voice better. You will notice that sometimes the device fails to recognize some of the commands you give it. It could be your voice or, accent is not being processed.

Fortunately, you can help Amazon Echo process your voice better by training it. You can do that by taking the following steps.

- You need to ensure that the microphone is on. If the light on top of the Echo device is blue, then it is ready. If it is red, it is on mute. You need to press the button with the microphone icon on top of the device.
- Try speaking to it. If it works, you may begin to train it to recognize your voice. (For the voice training feature, do not use the remote).
- You may begin training Echo to recognize your voice by going to the Amazon Echo app. Choose voice training located on the left panel.
- Select start and begin speaking out the phrases, so that the device can recognize your voice.
- You may now begin repeating the phrases as prompted. To repeat a phrase, click pause, then click on repeat phrase and speak out the phrase as indicated on the app.

IMPROVE EXPERIENCE

The Amazon Echo device connects to the cloud and will often try to make calculated guesses of what suits you. You can improve this by changing a few settings.

(a) Your Zip Code

Selecting the right Zip code will ensure you get more accurate information on traffic and weather information. You can change your Address Settings by simply going to settings >> [your device] >> Device location.

CUSTOMIZE YOUR MUSIC PLAYLIST

The device tries to find the best playlist based on what you've been playing or buying in the past. You can either add music to the playlist, or buy music from Amazon using the Wake word. However, this option is not fully functional. Amazon seems to be testing this feature.

AMAZON AND PURCHASES

Amazon will use your default payment options. However, you need to note that there are restrictions. These restrictions are mostly for those outside the US. There are also similar restrictions on the use of gift cards to buy through the Echo system. Before unboxing and making purchases, make a point of reading up to date information from the Amazon website. Amazon is still currently in the process of updating the information.

RESETTING THE DEVICE

It has been established that the device can freeze, or suffer some serious malfunctions on impact. This can happen when it accidentally falls. The Echo device may start playing music repeatedly. It may also freeze when playing music. The solution to this is to reset it.

Try unplugging the device from the wall. Let it remain unplugged for a few minutes then try again. Sometimes this will reset the device and it may be possible for it to function normally again.

Sometimes this may not be enough. The device may resort to freezing or playing music randomly without your input. You may need to unplug the device overnight. Let it stay unplugged for 12 hours without interruptions. In the morning, the device should be working.

IMPROVEMENTS TO AMAZON ECHO

Given that the device is still not yet available to buy directly, it may still be in its very early stages. As of now, the device still has limited capability. There may be a huge potential for growth. Amazon has indicated that there are several updates that are to be made to the system in the near future.

The device constantly connects to the cloud. It is possible for Amazon to make updates on the fly. Echo users may be waking up to find new features added through the cloud.

Some of the features that we could see in the near future is the ability for the device to recognize different voices living in the same house. The voice recognition technology may be quite sophisticated.

The solution may be to add a few more wake words beside "*Alexa*". This will help Echo create a different profile for each user. The different profiles could then help to create a better, more tailor made user experience for each user.

Amazon Echo may pioneer a new era of home tech systems. These systems may take voice commands for switching on the lights or controlling room temperature. Already there are smart people who have managed to create hacks that integrate Amazon Echo with home Web/Wi-Fi thermostat.

Amazon has made Apis available to the public. The source codes for Echo are also available on their website. With more devices designed to work with this kind of technology, the future is likely to get here faster than we had expected.

I want to thank you for purchasing and reading this book. I really hope you got a lot out of it.

If you enjoyed this book I would really appreciate it if you could leave me a positive review on Amazon.
I love getting feedback from my customers and reviews on Amazon really do make a difference. I read all my reviews and would really appreciate your thoughts.

Thanks so much.

Annabel Jacobs